THE GREATEST GREEK PHILOSOPHERS

PLATO

THE FATHER OF WESTERN PHILOSOPHY

LINDSAY ZOUBEK & ALEX SNIDERMAN

ROSEN PUBLISHING

NEW YORK

Published in 2016 by The Rosen Publishing Group, Inc.
29 East 21st Street, New York, NY 10010

Library of Congress Cataloging-in-Publication Data

Zoubek, Lindsay.
Plato : the father of western philosophy/Lindsay Zoubek and Alex Sniderman.—First Edition.
　　pages cm.—(The greatest Greek philosophers)
Includes bibliographical references and index.
ISBN 978-1-4994-6130-5 (library bound)
1. Plato. I. Title.
B393.Z68 2015
184—dc23

2014044178

Manufactured in the United States of America

CONTENTS

Plato is considered by many scholars and historians to be the father of the study of philosophy. The word "philosophy" is made up of two Greek words: *philos*, or "lover," and *sophia*, which means "wisdom." Most historians set Plato's birth in 428/427 BCE. Both of his parents came from distinguished families. His mother is thought to be related to a sixth century BCE Greek statesman and lyric poet named Solon. His father is believed to be a descendant of the kings of Athens and Messenia. Plato influenced every philosopher who came after him. He was a devoted pupil of Socrates's, the leading philosopher and teacher of the time. Unlike Socrates, Plato wrote down his ideas, which were influenced by Socrates and often featured Socrates as a character. It is from Plato's writings that students of philosophy have come to know Socrates's work.

The Athens of Plato's youth was a democracy and the center of Greek culture. Every male born in the city was considered a citizen and had the right to vote. Athens was also known for its strict class subdivisions, at the bottom of which were nearly 40,000 slaves. However, all citizens, regardless of their status or education, were allowed to vote. Theater and drama were also important aspects of life in Athens. Many of the plays written during Plato's time are still studied and performed today.

While philosophy, politics, theater, and drama were important parts of Plato's young life, political events also

Shown here is an oil painting of Plato from around 1475.

colored his experiences. From 431 to 404 BCE, Athens fought in the Peloponnesian War against Sparta. Plato himself may have had to participate in this war as a youth, though this remains unconfirmed. The war had its origins over fifty years earlier when a group of Greek city-states (including Athens, Chios, Samos, and Lesbos) held back an assault by the Persians in 480 BCE. These Greek city-states formed the Delian League in 478 BCE and built a navy to keep the Persians out. Athens was the most powerful member with the strongest navy, and the league came to be referred to as the Athenian Empire. The Peloponnesian War specifically began when the Athenian navy prevented Sparta's ally Corinth from invading Corcyra and attacked the Corinthian colony of Potidaea. Athens also refused to trade with another Spartan ally, Megara, effectively crippling Megara's economy. Athens was eventually defeated when Plato was about twenty-three years old. Plato and others blamed Athens's defeat on the city's focus on politics and culture. Eventually, the Spartan way of life would inspire Plato to formulate his thoughts on what he believed to be the ideal way of life. He would write about this in his famous work *The Republic*.

Plato distrusted the Athenian democracy of his childhood and believed that a civilized society functioned best when governed by a small group of wise men who would advise and make laws for the good of all. Many

This map depicts Greece at the beginning of the Peloponnesian War, c. 431 BCE.

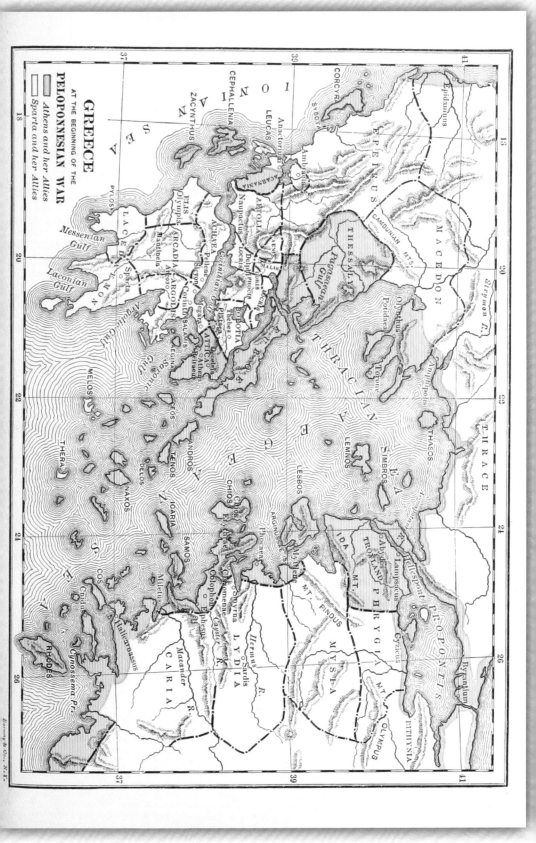

people who were part of the upper classes believed that Athens gave the poor and uneducated too much power by giving every citizen the right to vote. As part of that upper class, Plato also believed that power should be in the hands of only a few, who were both naturally disposed to making wise choices and also further trained to do so.

Plato's writings differ from those of other philosophers in that he wrote in the form of dialogues, or discussions between two or more characters. Most philosophers present their ideas and theories in essays in which they introduce and build upon their ideas in a series of paragraphs. Plato's dialogues discuss a variety of philosophical issues, including mathematics, science, ethics, death, and the universe.

The Republic, Plato's best known and, arguably, most important dialogue was written in the first half of the fourth century BCE, and it is divided into ten books that express some of Plato's most important ideas. Books 1–5 feature Plato's vision of the perfect government and his definition of justice. Books 6 and 7 explain what a philosopher is and introduce Plato's theory of ideas or forms. The last three, Books 8–10, focus on three practical forms of government and the positive and negative attributes of each. The main idea of Plato's work as a whole was to present the question "How best should a person live?" In Plato's dialogues, the character Socrates often questions people about what they claim to know. Socrates asks pointed questions that force others to rethink their beliefs, often causing them to doubt what they believed at the beginning. Historians

This color lithograph Epaminondas defends Pelopidas *shows the Theban general Epaminondas, who used battle tactics to break Spartan rule. The Athens of Plato's time was fraught with political and military upheaval.*

have attributed this to the real Socrates's style of debate, a tactic that made him unpopular and ultimately led to his death.

In 387 BCE, after several years of traveling to cities in southern Italy, Sicily, and Egypt, Plato returned to Athens and spent the rest of his life teaching and writing at the school he founded, which was called the Academy, located just outside the walls of Athens. Plato remained there until the end of his life, circa 348 BCE. The Academy lasted two more centuries under the direction of Plato's followers, until 83 BCE. It was revived in 410 CE and lasted a little over a hundred years until it was shut down by the Greek emperor Justinian I in 529 CE.

CHAPTER ONE

EARLY LIFE IN ATHENS

Most of the information concerning Plato is derived from his philosophical writings and the writings of his contemporaries. However, it is widely believed that he was born into a rich and powerful Athenian family in 428 or 427 BCE. He was named Aristocles at birth in honor of his grandfather. The name Plato was most likely a nickname from his youth because of his skill in wrestling. Plato, from the word *platon,* is thought to come from the Greek word for "flat" or "broad," a name well suited for Plato, with his broad shoulders.

ANCIENT ATHENS

Athens was the largest polis, or city-state, in ancient Greece. The city-states of ancient Greece were large metropolitan centers, which were part of the Greek nation. They had separate governments, laws, military, and cultural traditions. The word "metropolis"—which is used to describe large cities such as Athens today—comes from two Greek words: *metera*, meaning "mother," and *polis*, meaning "town." The term "metropolis" refers to any large town or urban place that is the cultural or economic center of its surrounding region. The metropolitan area of Athens also included Attica, a surrounding area outside the city.

Greek city-states had three different types of governments. The first was autocracy, in which one person, such as a king, had absolute power over the entire population. A second type of government for city-states was oligarchy, in which a small group of the rich and powerful made policy decisions for all. However, the Greeks are best remembered for inventing democracy, in which each citizen (males who had been born in the city-state) had the right to vote on policy.

Only about 40,000 people out of the total population of 150,000 Athenians were considered citizens. For example, women were completely excluded. None of the

The ruins of the Acropolis stand over modern Athens. The Acropolis— from the Greek akros *meaning "highest" and* polis, *which means "city"— was the site of several buildings during Plato's lifetime.*

free men (known as metics) who had immigrated from other countries or other parts of Greece in search of work were allowed to vote. However, they contributed to the economy through their employment and paid taxes to the city-state as did Athenian citizens. The enormous slave class, which made up close to a third of the city's population, was not paid for their work. As well, they did not pay taxes and were unable to participate in the political process.

Athens's location close to the sea made it a center for trade. Many Greek goods, including wines, pottery, and olive oil, were exported. Because much of Greece's land was mountainous and the soil conditions were poor, the Greeks imported most of their food. Grain was imported from the coastal region of the Black Sea (consisting of modern-day Turkey, Romania, Russia, Georgia, Bulgaria, and Ukraine). Other goods in short supply were meat, fish, and wood (for building ships), as well as slaves, who were often captured soldiers.

FAMILY LIFE

Plato's mother was related to Solon (638–558 BCE), a legendary Greek statesman. Solon was one of the seven sages who were famous for sayings such as "Know thyself" and "Nothing in excess"—two phrases still commonly heard today. Plato's father, Ariston, came from the family of Codrus, the last king of Athens. His father's side also claimed to be descended from the god Poseidon. Two of his relatives on his mother's side were members of the notorious Thirty Tyrants.

This detail from a piece of fifth-century BCE pottery shows a banquet. The Greeks followed a strict class hierarchy, with slaves at the bottom and wealthy families like Plato's at the top.

These were thirty upper-class men who ruled Athens after Sparta won the Peloponnesian War.

Historians believe that because Plato's family was wealthy and powerful, they probably had several slaves to help handle daily duties around the house. Because Athens had no sewer system, wealthy families had private wells. Less fortunate Athenians (or their slaves) had to visit a spring for fresh water and carry the water home in large ceramic jugs.

Homes of wealthier Athenians (like Plato's family) were usually built of stone. The poorer Athenians made their homes from mud-brick. These dwellings were easy prey for thieves and burglars, who were known as wall-diggers.

A typical Athenian man went to the agora or marketplace to buy food and other necessities for his household each morning. Women, unless they were forced to work outside the home to help support their families, were not allowed to venture out on their own. In wealthier homes, women were typically in charge of managing the slaves. Slaves took care of the smaller children as well as the housework.

RELIGION

The Greek religion was polytheistic, meaning that many different gods were worshipped. The Greek gods were said to live at the top of Mount Olympus, the highest mountain in Greece.

The Greeks considered the Twelve Olympian Gods (Zeus, Poseidon, Hera, Artemis, Hermes, Aphrodite,

This marble statue depicts the Greek goddess Artemis.

Apollo, Hades, Hephaestus, Ares, Athena, and Hestia) to be the most important. Nonetheless, many other gods, such as Dionysus, the god of wine, and Demeter, the goddess of harvest and fertility of the earth, were honored by the Greeks. Zeus was ruler of the heavens and the most powerful of the gods. He was responsible for justice, frequently settling quarrels with a hurled lightning bolt. Zeus's wife, Hera, was the goddess of marriage, and his brother Poseidon was god of the oceans. Some gods, like Aphrodite, the goddess of love, symbolized human emotions. The stories of Greek gods depicted them as a lively bunch. They were constantly embroiled in feuds and love affairs with each other—sometimes even with human beings.

The ancient Greeks also believed that certain people known as oracles had the ability to see into the future and understand things no other person could. The most famous Greek oracle was the oracle of Delphi. The temple at Delphi was built as a shrine to Apollo, the god of music. Apollo was believed to speak through the oracle. Seekers of truth would regularly journey to Delphi with questions, and the oracle would dispense answers and advice for a fee.

CULTURE IN ANCIENT GREECE

One of the ways the ancient Greeks honored their gods was by going to the theater to see plays. The entire cosmos was dramatized, with the gods above, a place of exile below, and in the center, a flat circle that represented Earth. A group of

THE HISTORY OF PHILOSOPHY

Philosophy is the study or pursuit of wisdom. The ancient Greeks were the fathers of what is called Western philosophy. It is known as Western philosophy because the ideas originated in Europe. Western philosophy encompasses many different disciplines, including science, religion, and politics.

Several civilizations produced great thinkers prior to ancient Greece, including the Hebrews, Arabs, and Egyptians. However, before the Greek philosophers, there were no experiments or measured tests to prove an assertion. A philosopher could consider a question or problem such as why olives grew in one place better than in another, decide on an answer, and declare it to be the truth without any supporting proof. The Greeks were the first to use proofs to support their conclusions.

twelve to fifty people performed in the center circle, which was called the orchestra. The Greek word *orkheisthai* means "to dance" and *tra* denotes place, so it roughly translates to "the dancing place." The two or three principal characters moved either with the gods or in exile. The action was commented on and sung about by the chorus.

Comedy and tragedy, the two varieties of drama invented by the ancient Greeks, are still considered the cornerstones of the modern theater. Drama and poetry were celebrated with great festivals and contests that went on for days, and at the end, a winner was given a prize. Plato himself participated in several poetry contests before deciding to focus his energies on philosophy.

The arts of ancient Greece are still appreciated and studied today—especially sculpture and pottery. Greek pottery illustrated everything from scenes of everyday ancient life to religious or historical events. Sculpture was also very important. Many statues and monuments were created in honor of gods, famous heroes, or statesmen.

The architecture of ancient Greece featured many formidable and lasting monuments to commemorate the gods and their civilization. Of all of the Greek arts, examples of architecture have survived most intact. The most famous Greek monument is probably the Acropolis, a collection of temples built to honor the gods of Olympus. On the highest point of the Acropolis stands the Parthenon, a temple honoring Athena,

The theater of Epidaurus in Greece was built in the fourth century BCE. It seats up to 15,000 people and is famous for its acoustics.

the Greek goddess of wisdom for whom the city of Athens was named. Ruins of the acropolis are still standing.

PLATO AS A YOUNG MAN

Because Plato came from a wealthy family, it is most likely that he was well educated. He probably studied with private tutors in his home, learning how to read, write, and play music. When boys in ancient Greece were older, they were given physical training and exercise in the gymnasium, which set the stage for military training.

The first great Greek civilization was that of the Mycenaeans (1600–1100 BCE), whose times were recounted in the works of Homer, a Greek historian. Homer lived sometime in the eighth century BCE— about four hundred years before Plato. The epic poetry of Homer's *The Iliad* and *The Odyssey* recounted the deeds of legendary heroes Achilles and Odysseus. These stories, which remain classics of Greek literature and civilization, were essential reading for young Greeks.

The Olympic Games originated in Greece. Though Plato was a highly regarded wrestler, he never competed in the Olympics. However, historians have never been able to determine why this was. He did, however, participate in the Isthmian Games, an ancient Greek festival of athletic and musical competitions in honor of the sea god Poseidon.

Though Plato's family background suggested that, ultimately, he would probably be involved in politics, his interest in philosophy, fueled by his teacher Socrates,

This thirteenth-century illustration shows Socrates writing to Plato.

turned him to a life of teaching and studying rather than public service.

OTHER PHILOSOPHERS OF PLATO'S TIME

Plato came to his conclusions based on the ideas of those who came before him, building on Socrates's method of questioning and refuting those past philosophers with whose ideas he disagreed. Plato also influenced modern philosophy, as he was the first to write down his works. Socrates, for example, never did. Everything that is known of Socrates's work is based on Plato's writings. Plato also challenged the work of other philosophers.

Protagoras believed that knowledge was something relative, or unique to each person. For example, one person might huddle under blankets saying that a 50 degree Fahrenheit (10 degree Celsius) day was freezing, while on that same day, another person might decide to wear very little clothing and complain about the heat. According to Protagoras, both conclusions were true. Protagoras is well-known for saying "Man is the measure of all things." In other words, each person's individual experience teaches him to make judgments about the world.

Another contemporary of Plato's was the mathematician and philosopher Theodorus. In the field of mathematics, Theodorus is best known for his work with square roots. Philosophically, Theodorus believed that in order to understand the world one had to experience it through the five senses of smell, sight, taste, touch, or hearing. Knowing the world and perceiving, or experiencing, the world was the same thing.

Unlike these philosophers, Plato's philosophy centered on the idea of an unchanging and perfect form that united all things. What made a person good was whatever enabled him or her to live good lives. Likewise, what made a scale good was whatever enabled it to measure well. The form itself—the thing that makes everything good—was true reality, not the things themselves. Plato later moved away from the idea that it was possible for human minds to know and understand forms without error. The idea of forms clashed with Protagoras's theory of relativism as well as with Theodorus's belief that experience equals knowledge.

Plato developed the theory of forms because of another philosopher, Heraclitus. Heraclitus believed that the world was in a state of constant flux, or change. He believed people's ideas changed as they learned new information and had different life experiences. Accordingly, his work is similar to both Protagoras's belief in relativism and Theodorus's idea of individual experience. As Heraclitus stated, "No man steps in the same river twice." Plato's opposition to the idea of a mercurial world that changed based on the person experiencing it led to his forms. He argued that if everything was in a state of constant change, no one would be able to talk to each other because the actual names of people and objects—the entire language itself—would be constantly changing. Each person would only be able to understand language individually.

This is a bust of Heraclitus of Ephesus.

Hence, communication would be nearly impossible, as no one could understand anyone else.

THE THIRTY TYRANTS

When Plato was a young man, Athens was defeated by the southern Greek city-state of Sparta in the Peloponnesian War. Spartan society was focused on building military might and maintaining its power. When Spartan boys were seven years old, they were taken from their families and sent to live in barracks where they would begin military training. As in Athens, the number of slaves (known in Sparta as helots) greatly outnumbered the free citizens. The Spartan citizens treated helots with cruelty. They forced them to serve in the Spartan army but denied them any rights in the government.

When Athens was defeated by Sparta, the Spartans tore down the city walls and installed a pro-Spartan oligarchy in which a group of thirty rich and powerful Athenians governed the polis. Among these thirty Athenians were Plato's relatives, Critias and Charmides. The Thirty Tyrants, as they were known, often executed their enemies and forced many to flee the city in fear. Many enemies of the Thirty Tyrants who escaped Athens tried to raise armies to drive them out and restore democratic rule in the city. In 403 BCE, the democratic opposition managed to run the Thirty Tyrants out of town. As a result, the Spartans, who were no longer worried about Athens as a threat, allowed democratic rule to be reinstated in 402 BCE.

The cruelty with which the Thirty Tyrants governed Athens completely disgusted Plato. It turned him more completely toward philosophy and Socrates.

SOCRATES

Socrates was born in Athens around the year 470 BCE, the son of a midwife and a stonemason. Socrates' method of teaching, which was revolutionary at the time, is still in use today. The Socratic method, as it is known, is used to direct a student toward deducing an answer by presenting the student with a series of questions. For example, a teacher would ask students to provide the definition of justice. Perhaps a student would respond with the answer that justice is a decision by a court of law. The teacher would then ask students if court cases were always decided in a just or fair way. The students might answer, no, not in every single case. This contradiction would lead the group to examine other situations and ideas and how each related to justice. Ideally, the students and teacher would ultimately be able to eliminate conflicting ideas until a single definition of justice could be agreed upon.

SOCRATES THE TEACHER

Although Socrates was a stonemason by trade and had a wife and three sons to support, he is thought to have spent most of his time engaging in philosophical

This statue of Socrates stands in front of the National Academy of Athens.

discussions in the agora, or marketplace, of Athens. He was not at all interested in money and did not charge for his teaching. He was concerned only with the study of philosophy. Socrates was an enemy of the Sophists, teachers who traveled through Greece teaching classes for a fee. The Sophists' philosophy stated that the important thing in life was getting what you wanted and persuading others to give it to you. In contrast, Socrates thought the role of knowledge was to learn how to be a good person.

SOCRATES THE SKILLED DEBATER

When Plato met Socrates, Plato believed he had finally found a subject—philosophy—to which he could devote his life. He became Socrates' most famous student and constant companion for the next nine years. Plato tried to learn all he could from Socrates. As a result, Socrates would become his most influential teacher.

Socrates believed that gaining knowledge about oneself and the world was key to self-improvement. Although he was humble about the limits of his own knowledge, through a process of continual questioning of issues, he believed that it was possible to live the life of a good person. Socrates became famous in Athens for his ability to expose people's lack of knowledge. As a result of his debating skill and intellect, people crowded around him to hear what he had to say.

SOCRATES'S TRIAL AND DEATH

After years spent teaching in the streets of Athens, in 399 BCE, Socrates was formally charged with corrupting the youth of Athens. Those in power believed that Socrates's constant questioning was influencing the people of Athens in the wrong ways. Socrates protested the charge, telling the court he was nothing more than a seeker of truth who wanted to find a true way to live. Despite Socrates's protests, he was sentenced to death.

Plato took his teacher's death very hard. He realized that as a friend of Socrates's, he was also in danger. He and many other philosophers left Athens shortly after Socrates's death. Plato did not return for the next twelve years.

CHAPTER TWO

PLATO'S EDUCATION IN PHILOSOPHY

Plato moved just twenty miles (thirty-two kilometers) away to a neighboring territory called Megara. Despite its close proximity to Athens, Plato remained there safely for the next three years. Also living there at the time was his friend Euclides and several other Socratic followers who had also fled Athens. During this time, Plato began to write his first works: *Apology*, *Crito*, *Euthyphro*, and *Phaedo*.

Plato's philosophical writings are noteworthy because of the way he wrote them. His are in the form of dialogues. Most philosophical works of his contemporaries

This manuscript page is from Plato's The Dialogues. *It was dedicated to Lorenzo the Magnificent, the head of the Medici family, c. 1480. The Medici family owned many important literary works, including some by Plato.*

MARSILII·FICINI·PREFATIO·AD·MAGNIFI
CV VIRV LAVRETIVM MEDICE IN DIALOGOS PLA
TONIS DE PHILOSOPHIA EGRECO IN LTINV PEV TDVCO˜S

DIVINA PROVIDENTIA FORTITER ATTIGES
omia suauiterq; disponens Magnanime Laurenti statuit
religione sanctam non solum ppheris et sibyllis sacrisq; arma
re doctoribus: uerx et pia quadam elegantiq; philosophia singu
lariter exornare. Vt ipa pietas omnium origo bonor˜ tã secu
ra tandé inter omnis sapientiæ & eloquentiæ pfessores incedet
q˜ tuta inter domesticos conquiescit. Oportebat. x. religione
quæ unica est ad felicitaté uia non rudioribs tm hominibz uerx etiam peritio
ribs cõmunem fore: qua qdem duce omnis ad beatitudiné cui˜ gra nati sumus: et
ad quam consequendam comuni studio laboramvs: facilius tuti˜q; puenire possem˜.
Itaq; devs omnipotes statutis teporibs diuini˜ Platonis animv ab alto demisit: uita
ingenio eloqoq; mirabili religione sacram apd omnis gentes illustratvrv. Cvm u˜o
ad hæc vsq; secula sol platonicvs non dum palam latinis gentibz oriret. Cosm˜
Italiæ decvs et insignis pietate uir platonicam lucem religioni admodvm salutare
a 6recis ad Latinos propagare contendens sue potissimvm intra suos lares plu
rimvm educatvm tanto operi destinauit. Ego aut˜ ersi a tenera ætate nominis
platonici cvltor: ré tm adeo grauem non meis qdem sed aut tvi Cosmi psperis au
spicijs svm aggressvs: sperans diuinam opem tam necessario tamq; pio officio non
defutvram. Hac ergo iprimis spe dvctvs Academiam svm ingressvs: decemq; ex
ea Platonis nostri dialogos Cosmo prius q˜ natura concederet Latinos feci. Post ei˜
obitvm patri tuo Petro prestantissimo uiro dialogos nouem legendos dedi. Postq˜ u˜o
Petrvs e vita decessit Fortuna preclaris sæpe operibz inuida inuictvm me a tradu
ctionis officio distrahebat. Uerx tv & religionis cvltor et phiæ patronvs me ad
inceptvm omni fauore et auxilio reuocasti. Quaobre ad institutvm munvs feli
cibus itervm auspicijs svm regressvs. Heq; traduxi tantvm: uerx et ptim argv
mentis mentem pstrinxi platonicam: ptim quoad potui breuibus comentarijs expli
caui. Opus itaq; totv diuino auxilio iam absolutvm tibi libentissime dedico. Ad
quem illa etiam quæ matoribs tuis inscripta sunt: iure hereditario ptinent: Vt
rvm pfecto auitæ paternæq; in patria colenda uirtutis herede. Leges aut in
ter dialogos funebrem Platonis orationem pio fratri tvo Iuliano dicatam. Prete
rea vbi ad librvm de regno pueneris: videbis Federicvm vrbinatem ducem
eo die a me honoratvm: quo ipe tuas ædes honorifice salutauit. Non solvm u˜o
septe atq; triginta libri: qui solo tvo insigniti sunt titulo: sed cuncti denuq; tvi
sunt: cnqdem omis tui gratia sunt absoluti: atq; ego svm tuus. Heq; u˜o me
platonicvm in his libris stilvm omnino expressisse profiteor: Neq; rurs˜ a bullo
quis admodvm doctiore vnq˜ exprimi posse confido. Stilv inq˜ no tam humano
eloquio q˜ diuino oraculo simile: sæpe quidé tonante alti˜: sæpe u˜o nectarea
suauitate manante: Semper aut archana cælestia cõplectente. Profecto que

and those who followed him were written in the form of essays. Plato's work is structured much more like drama. In his dialogues, two or more characters discuss issues back and forth, eventually coming to a final conclusion. Plato's dialogues often feature Socrates questioning the views of other participants until he establishes that they were not entirely correct.

WHOSE PHILOSOPHY?

It's not entirely known whether the views expressed by Socrates as a character are truly his, or if Plato used the character of Socrates as a vehicle to put forth his own ideas. The truth is probably somewhere in the middle.

In his dialogues, Plato presents Socrates as both an example of an honest person whom others should follow as well as a provocative thinker who would go to almost any length to make his opponents admit they were wrong. Because of the lack of historical information on the lives of both Plato and Socrates, it's impossible to determine what these two men were like in real life. The only conclusions that can be drawn about Socrates's come from Plato's work and the work of other writers. Two of these were the playwright Aristophanes, who featured Socrates as a character in his work, and Socrates' former pupil Xenophon, who also wrote in defense of his teacher as Plato later did.

Plato's first works are based on trying to prove that Socrates's search for truth was the best way to live—the way that all people should live. Plato found it very difficult to face the idea that although Socrates had lived what Plato considered an honest life, he ended up being put to death by his government.

APOLOGY

One of Plato's first works is *Apology*, in which he reconstructs Socrates's entire defense during his trial. This is the most accurate record of the Socratic method in action. Throughout *Apology*, Socrates addresses the jury and prosecutors in the courtroom.

Socrates's defense tactic in *Apology* is to try and prove to the court that instead of being guilty of corruption, he was actually providing a public service to Athenians by helping them find the truth, or more specifically, aiding them to come to a realization of what they really knew. In *Apology*, Socrates recalls his friend Chaerephon's trip to the oracle at Delphi. Chaerephon asked the oracle who was the wisest mortal, or human being. The oracle responded that "no man is wiser" than Socrates. This completely shocked Socrates and compelled him to undertake the mission of finding a man who was wiser than he was.

Since the oracle at Delphi was believed to be infallible, or unable to make a mistake, Socrates could not deny her statement. However, Socrates still thought of himself as ignorant. He believed that human beings cannot truly know anything worthwhile. Socrates felt that the only knowledge or wisdom he truly had was that he freely admitted what he did not know. The only fair test, then, would be to try and find someone wiser.

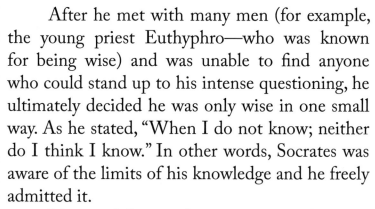

After he met with many men (for example, the young priest Euthyphro—who was known for being wise) and was unable to find anyone who could stand up to his intense questioning, he ultimately decided he was only wise in one small way. As he stated, "When I do not know; neither do I think I know." In other words, Socrates was aware of the limits of his knowledge and he freely admitted it.

Many of Socrates's opponents refused to admit that they might not be wise until Socrates was able to prove it. In *Apology*, Socrates told the jury that he felt he was chosen for the mission of showing people the true depth of their knowledge. As he stated:

The god has placed me in the city. I never cease to rouse each and every one of you, to persuade and reproach you all day long and everywhere I find myself in your company.

Socrates saw himself much like a priest who takes a vow of poverty in order to spend his time ministering to others. Believing that the most important thing a person could do is find the truth, in *Apology*, Socrates noted, "The unexamined life is

This nineteenth-century illustration shows Socrates on trial for corrupting youth and for impiety.

not worth living." He felt that through this process of questioning he would be able to help people find the true way to live. As he continued:

> I go around seeking out anyone, citizen or stranger, whom I think wise. Then if I do not think he is, I come to the assistance of the god and show him that he is not wise.

Socrates defended himself against the charge that he was corrupting young people. He told the court that he never forced his ideas or beliefs on anyone. Instead, he simply searched for the

These shards of pottery were used as voting ballots around 482 BCE.

truth and anyone who wanted to follow him was welcome to do so.

SOCRATES'S IMPACT

In Plato's *Apology*, the philosopher attempts to describe the speech that Socrates gave at his trial. It is not known how closely his transcription came to the original. Socrates believed that the negative views toward him were because he would willingly cross-examine his fellow citizens and show that they were not as secure in their knowledge as they believed. As a result, those people grew to despise him. He added that it was only the young and wealthy who had the time to follow his teachings, and then question their elders, effectively making it seem as if he had corrupted the youth of Athens.

Socrates believed that the real problem was that the elders merely did not want to be questioned. Many of them thought that being queried by their children eroded their status as parents or authority figures. Socrates pointed out in *Apology* that those who were questioned "are angry, not with themselves but with me." Socrates felt that the anger these people felt at being taken to task by their children led them to use him as a scapegoat. Instead, he felt they should have used the opportunity for moral reflection of themselves. They concluded that if Socrates was disposed of, they would not have to face the fact that they may not be as smart as they would like to think they are.

Although Plato's *Apology* indicates that Socrates defended himself admirably, the court still found him

PYTHAGORAS AND ARCHYTAS

The Greek mathematician and philosopher Pythagoras was one of the most important influences on Plato's work besides Socrates. Like Socrates, Pythagoras did not write down his ideas. What we know of him comes from the writings of the mathematicians and philosophers who came after him. Pythagoras lived c. 570–495 BCE.

Pythagoras believed that numbers were the key to learning the truth about the world. A famous saying attributed to Pythagoras is "All is number." He theorized that numbers provided the basis for the explanation of relationships in various disciplines, including mathematics and music. Pythagoras was the first person to identify the reason certain musical notes sounded good together.

He is best known for the Pythagorean theorem, which states that the square of the hypotenuse (the side opposite the right angle of a right triangle) is equal to the sum of the squares of the other two sides.

During his travels away from Athens, Plato met a Pythagorean and philosopher named Archytas, who was equally as involved in politics as he was in philosophy. Archytas gave Plato a concrete example of how a person could be both a philosopher and a ruler—an ideal Plato would try to realize for the rest of his life.

guilty of the charge of corrupting the young. As a result, they sentenced him to death. As was the Athenian custom, the accused person was allowed to propose an alternative to the punishment given by the court. Socrates reasoned that because his aims had been to make Athenians aware of the truth about their lives and work to be better people, he was actually performing a public service. Socrates thought that instead of a death penalty for performing good work, he should receive free meals for the rest of his life. One last option Socrates brought forth was the possibility of paying a fine. However, as he admitted that he had no wealth to speak of, he could only pay a fine of one mina, which amounted to about twenty-five dollars.

The court voted for the last time, and the verdict to put Socrates to death stood unchanged. As written in Plato's *Apology*, Socrates reacted to the decision by stating, "It is not hard to avoid death . . . it is much more difficult to avoid wickedness." He went on to predict that killing him would not destroy his ideas. Socrates told the court that his followers and fellow philosophers would come forward in his place and continue his work. As he stated in *Apology*, "You are wrong if you believe that by killing people you will prevent anyone from reproaching you for not living in the right way." He continued, saying that he did not fear death and looked forward to the next world.

Pythagoras draws the proof for his theorem in the sand.

Socrates's follower and friend Crito pleaded with Socrates to escape Athens. However, Socrates soundly refused. Although he disagreed with the court's decision, Socrates felt that to escape would be breaking the law. Also, such an act would damage the integrity of the honest life he had lived. Even if the court was wrong, he was willing to abide by the decision because he felt that to disobey the law would be worse than death. Accordingly, he willingly drank the poisonous hemlock he was given. He died surrounded by many of his followers, including Plato. Eventually, Plato would write about his mentor's death in his work *Phaedo*.

PLATO CAPTURES THE LAST DAYS OF SOCRATES

In addition to *Apology*, three other dialogues Plato wrote—*Euthyphro*, *Crito*, and *Phaedo*—discuss the last days of Socrates's life. In each dialogue, Plato further explored Socrates's ideas, using his trial and death to show Socrates's integrity as an honest person who was in search of the truth. Socrates paid the ultimate price for the truth—his life—which he gave without complaint and with great dignity. In two of the four early dialogues—*Apology* and *Euthyphro*—Plato gives Socrates the role of a smart aleck who is aware that he won't be getting the answers he desires from the person he's questioning. Socrates is not mean-spirited, only disappointed in his inability to get the response he's after, and is merely trying to make people think, as he states in *Apology*.

THE NATURE OF PIETY

Euthyphro features Socrates trying to discover and under-stand the nature of piety, or being true and respectful of the gods. In the dialogue, Plato places Socrates in the company of Euthyphro, a young priest who, despite his standing as a religious leader, is unable to give Socrates a true definition of piety.

Plato sets the scene with Socrates making his way to his trial. On the way to court, Socrates meets Euthyphro, who is involved in a different trial. Euthyphro tells Socrates he is trying his own father for murder. A servant in his father's house killed one of the family's slaves. His father tied up the killer and left him in a ditch while he sent for instructions from the priest as to what to do with him. While the messenger was gone, the killer died of exposure. Euthyphro's actions angered many Athenians. They said it was impious, or against the will of the gods, to prosecute one's own father.

Plato leads Socrates to engage Euthyphro in a discussion of the nature of piety. Socrates believes that as a priest, Euthyphro has special insight into the true definition of piety. Euthyphro tells Socrates that "what is dear to the gods is pious, what is not is impious." Plato has Socrates point out to Euthyphro that the Greek gods are not perfect beings. In many religions, such as Christianity, Islam, and Judaism, it is believed that the gods are perfect. However, the Olympians fought frequently among themselves, had many petty jealousies, and sometimes engaged in romantic affairs with human beings.

By pointing out the faults of the gods, Plato showed that because the Olympian gods disagreed over many things, what one god believed to be pious, another might not agree with. This meant that the definition of piety that Euthyphro gave Socrates did not hold true. Euthyphro then brings up the idea that if the gods love something, they love it because of its piety; in other words, that it was not pious just because they loved it.

At this point, Euthyphro is drawn in to Socrates's web of questioning and begins searching for

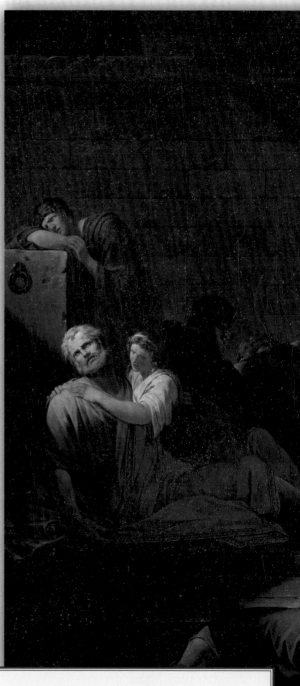

The Death of Socrates *was painted by Jean-François-Pierre Peyron in 1786.*

any way out of the situation. Socrates states that if he can prove to the court that he has acquired real knowledge of piety, the court might have mercy on him. As such, he might be able to "escape [prosecutor] Meletus'indictment by showing him that [he] had acquired wisdom in divine matters from Euthyphro." Euthyphro eventually tells Socrates's he doesn't have the time to give him a true definition of piety and heads to his trial. Unfortunately, Socrates is forced to do the same.

As in *Apology*, in *Euthyphro*, Plato allows Socrates to present a logical argument about his subject, which his opponent is not able to contradict. In both dialogues, Socrates's opponents come to their own conclusions without paying much attention to Socrates's exposure of the flaws in their thinking. In allowing Socrates to put forth ideas that contradict those of men like Euthyphro the priest and Meletus the prosecutor (who were thought to be wise), Plato seems to be saying that many people in powerful positions may not be willing to listen to ideas that contradict their own—no matter how much sense these ideas make.

UNJUST PUNISHMENT IN *CRITO*

Plato's depiction of Socrates in *Crito* presents a slightly different view of the man who was sentenced to death.

Shown here is a sculpture by Jean-Baptiste Roman of Cato the Younger, a Roman politician and statesman, reading Phaedo *by Plato before committing suicide.*

In *Apology*, in which Socrates suggests that his punishment be free meals for life in return for his service to Athens, he is presented as thoughtful, wise, and willing to die even though he believes himself to be innocent—all just to prove his point that by honestly following the laws of Athens, he will remain innocent and his opponents guilty.

Crito takes place in Socrates's prison cell as he awaits execution. In this dialogue, Plato illustrates Socrates's honesty and integrity by having him refuse the option of an easy escape from Athens and, hence, from death. In an unusual twist of fate, Socrates's execution is put off for a month due to a religious mission in

Socrates talks before a group of men with the figure of justice behind him.

which a Greek ship is sent on a return journey to the island of Delos. During the voyage, no executions are allowed to take place. At the time of Crito and Socrates's conversation, the ship is returning to Athens. It is during this time that Crito tries to convince Socrates that it is his last chance to escape his death sentence, but Socrates will hear nothing of it.

Crito tells Socrates, "I do not think that what you are doing is right, to give up your life when you can save it," but Socrates soundly refuses Crito's invitation to escape. Socrates expresses to Crito, "One should never do wrong in return, nor injure any man, whatever injury one has suffered at his hands." Socrates feels that trying to escape his punishment would be ignoring all the laws of Athens. Accordingly, he tells Crito that if people begin to ignore laws, society will crumble. Though he calmly refuses to believe that what he has done is wrong, Socrates does not deny the Athenian court's right to order that he be put to death.

By presenting Socrates as a man who'd rather die than go against the laws of his homeland, Plato once again depicts Socrates's strength of character in the face of unjust opposition. The Socrates Plato presents in *Crito* refuses to think of himself or his own safety. Instead, he is concerned only with living an honest and just life, even if it comes at the expense of his own life. He states that running away would "strengthen the conviction of the jury that they passed the right sentence" on Socrates—that to flee would be admitting his guilt. Crito finally realized that his friend's resolve is absolute and that no matter what he says, he will not be able to persuade him to save his life by leaving Athens and hence avoiding his death.

LAST MOMENTS OF DIGNITY IN *PHAEDO*

In *Phaedo*, Socrates continues to philosophize with his students and friends up to the end of his life. Despite his difficult manner when questioning people, the Socrates portrayed by Plato in *Phaedo* is a wise gentleman who went to his death with no regrets or sadness. Of course, those around him are terribly upset. Socrates shows such peace in the face of death that even the officer who comes to administer the poison to him is moved by his dignity. The officer tells Socrates that he was "the noblest, the gentlest, and the best man who has ever come here." Socrates takes the cup of poison, drinks it, and dies. His followers openly weep around him.

CHAPTER THREE

A DEPARTURE FROM SOCRATES

In *Phaedo*, Plato began to explore the idea that the world was divided into two parts: the world that was perceived through our senses and a more perfect world of ideas, only reachable through thought. *Phaedo* also marked the end of Plato's exploration of his teacher Socrates. His most famous work, *The Republic*, continued the ideas that he presented of a divided world in *Phaedo* and explored his own theories of knowledge.

Plato called these perfect ideas forms. He believed that in their daily lives, humans do not directly experience forms. Instead, they experience visible, material objects. Plato suggested that these ordinary objects are imperfect copies of the perfect forms. Philosophy students of Plato's

Here you can see a page from the oldest surviving manuscript of The Republic *by Plato.*

were taught that the objects of the world are not completely unique and that each object has various elements that can be categorized in various groupings. There are categories, or forms, for objects, such as animals, and there are forms for concepts, such as beauty and justice. Plato believed that the forms cause objects to be what they are. For example, the form of a lion makes a lion the animal that we perceive through our senses. Though objects, such as a lion, can die, and what we may consider beautiful may change, the forms never change. They are eternal and remain perfect. Socrates says in the Republic that people who cannot see the forms are like people who are dreaming but think they are awake. Only the philosopher can know the truth about ordinary experience because a philosopher can see the dream for what it is.

PLATO'S ALLEGORY OF THE CAVE

In Book 7 of *The Republic*, Plato uses an example of people who are forced to live their entire lives chained together inside a cave and unable to move to explain his idea that normal reality is like a dream.

> Picture human beings living in an underground dwelling like a cave, with a long entrance open to the light, as wide as the cave. They are there

In Plato's Republic, *he describes Socrates's allegory of the cave, in which man is compared to creatures who live in a dark cave and see only the shadows of reality.*

La Caverne de Platon. — Composition et dessin de Chevignard.

from childhood, with chains on their legs and their necks so that they stay where they are and can only see in front of them, unable to turn their heads because of the fetters. Light comes from a fire which is burning higher up and some way behind them; and also higher up, between the first and the prisoners, there is a road along which a low wall is built, like the screen in front of puppeteers above which they show their puppets.

Since the people in the cave cannot see anything except for the shadows, they believe that these shadows are real. The prisoners think there is nothing else. They do not even know that these are shadows since they have never seen the puppets or the light behind them. In constructing this allegory, Plato is saying that people who do not understand the forms are living in a sort of prison of the mind. In this prison, what the prisoners think of as the real world of experience is only a projection of something else. The shadows are to the puppets as the visible objects of ordinary experience are to the forms.

However, the world of the cave is more complex than this since there are two sets of images and originals in it. Plato writes of a prisoner who is freed from his bonds and leaves the cave. On his way out, he sees and experiences many things. First, he sees the puppets and the fire that create the shadows on the wall of the cave. As he exits the cave, he is blinded by the brightness of the sun. Slowly, as his eyes become accustomed to the light, he is able to distinguish reflections and the shadows of things outside of the cave. Ultimately, he becomes aware of his surroundings and the sun that provides light. He also recognizes that the puppets are copies of the things outside of the cave.

Once the prisoner takes all of this in, he begins to understand that the objects outside of the cave are the source of the things inside the cave. The puppets are modeled on the objects outside of the cave, and the shadows are shaped like the puppets. As a result, the prisoner can understand that just as the shadows in the cave are images of the puppets, everything in the cave is like an image of what is outside of the cave. (The shadows, then, are not even like visible objects, but more like images on a television or movie screen. We would be just like the prisoners if we watched a movie and thought it was reality that we were watching instead of images of and stories created about the world.) In this way, the world inside the cave represents the visible world and the world outside the cave represents the world of ideas.

The fire allows the freed prisoner to see the shadows and the puppets represent the sun in the ordinary world. In the same way, the sun outside the cave represents the object that allows us to see the forms. But what is this sun really? What makes it possible to know the forms that stand behind the world we see around us?

THE IDEA OF THE GOOD

Plato states in *The Republic*, "What provides truth to the things known and gives the power to the one who knows

An obverse (the heads side of a coin) shows Helios, the sun god. This coin hails from the second century BCE.

is the idea of the good." Truth is like light in that it explains what we can understand. In other words, what Plato is defining as the good is the source of our ability to comprehend. To know what is good or what is best would be to know why things in the world are the way they are. For example, in *Euthyphro*, Socrates asks Euthyphro, a young priest, to define piety, but Euthyphro is unable to do so. Plato asserts that if Euthyphro truly understood the form of the good, he would have no trouble giving Socrates an exact definition of piety. According to Plato, the form of the good is the basis for understanding all other ideas.

To know and understand the form of the good provides one with the tools to find the truth in every idea and object. Being able to do so is also the key to the ability to live an honest life. However, Plato also warns that while both knowledge and truth are effects of the good, they should not be confused with the form of the good. According to Plato, that would be like confusing the sun's light with the sun itself. Sunlight is only a product of the sun, just as knowledge and truth are products of the good. The good is the underlying basic idea that makes all other knowledge possible.

Plato believed that all human beings are born with the capacity to understand the form of the good. Plato states that "this power is in the soul of each" person. However, just as the prisoner's journey out of the cave is a difficult and painful one, so is the effort to understand the good. Instead of needing to be educated or instructed on what is true, Plato felt that people needed to have their minds turned toward the good, since this is the source of all truth and knowledge. In other words, being instructed about what is true is not enough. What is really needed is a complete change of the soul "until it is able to endure looking at that which is and brightest part of that which is. And we affirm that this is the good." Plato is suggesting that everyone has the ability to understand the world—and truth—by turning toward the good. This understanding would enable people not only to "see" the forms that stand behind the visible world but also to understand why the forms themselves are what they are.

PLATO AND KING DIONYSIUS I

During his travels to the island of Sicily, Plato became acquainted with Dion, the brother-in-law of the ruler of Syracuse. Syracuse's king, Dionysius I, was a great soldier and military leader who built his kingdom into a military powerhouse by using brilliant strategy to crush his opponents. An admirer of the arts and philosophy, Dionysius I was well-known for his own poetry and drama. One of his plays won an award at an Athenian festival, though the rumor was that the prize was given only to prevent Dionysius I from attacking Plato's home city.

Dion convinced Plato that Dionysius I might have a place in his court for a philosopher. Plato was eager to give the position a try. Unfortunately for Plato, Dionysius I, like the Athenians who tried Socrates in court, did not take kindly to Plato's use of the Socratic method of questioning. The two men disagreed about many ideas, and

This coin displays the head of Dionysius I, the tyrant of Syracuse.

PHILOSOPHER-KINGS IN HISTORY

Plato's ideas influenced several world leaders centuries after his death. Roman emperor Marcus Aurelius, who ruled from 161 to 180 CE, is probably the first philosopher-king as defined by Plato. He studied philosophy heavily and

This statue is of Marcus Aurelius, the Roman emperor from 161 to 180 CE.

This statue of Matthias Corvinus stands in Romania. Corvinus was a ruler who was well-known for being wise and just.

wrote *Mediations*, a treatise on his ideas about philosophy. Matthias Corvinus, king of Hungary from 1458 until his death in 1490, was well educated and noted for his support of the arts. He also encouraged the discussion of philosophy in his court. Upon his death, the saying "Matthias is dead—justice is lost" became popular.

However, Plato's ideas did not always generate well-loved leaders. Joseph Stalin, the Communist leader of the Soviet Union from the mid-1920s until his death in 1953, and Adolf Hitler, leader of the German Nazi Party, were both influenced by Plato's ideas about leadership and glorification of country over all else.

ultimately, their disagreements ended when Dionysius I accused Plato of being an old fool. Plato shot back that Dionysius I was acting like a tyrant by asking him to come to Syracuse and instruct him in philosophy only to ignore all Plato's teaching and advice. In a fit of anger, Dionysius I had Plato thrown in jail and then deported from Syracuse on a Spartan ship. Dionysius told the ship's captain to sell Plato as a slave in the market on the island of Aegina.

When Plato was on the auction block at the market, a friend and fellow philosopher named Anniceris recognized him and purchased him. He immediately set Plato free and sent him back to Athens.

THE PHILOSOPHER-KING

The time that Plato spent with Dionysius I led him to think about what kind of a society would be best and how this ideal society should be governed. Plato concluded that this ideal society would best be governed by a capable leader who had a complete understanding of the form of the good. In much of *The Republic*, Plato discusses what the perfect society would entail and a way of living that would provide the good life to all of its inhabitants. In *The Republic*, Plato states, "Unless the philosophers rule as kings or those now called kings and chiefs genuinely and adequately philosophize . . . there will be no rest from ills for the cities . . . nor I think for human kind."

Dionysius I is a bad ruler in Plato's ideal society. According to Plato, to rule means to set things in order according to what is best. This requires an understanding of the good. Although the ruler of Syracuse was a great military leader and could command large numbers of people, he did not truly understand the form of the good. When Plato pointed this out to the king, Dionysius I was unable to tolerate Plato's criticism of him. Plato believed his philosopher-king would have an understanding of the form of the good so he would not feel threatened by someone trying to prove him wrong.

CHAPTER FOUR

THE ACADEMY AND PLATO'S LAST TEACHINGS

W hen Plato returned to Athens in 387 BCE, he founded a school known as the Academy. He spent the rest of his life at the Academy, where he taught, studied, and continued writing. Plato believed that the only way to respond to what had happened to Socrates was for him to train young people to be statesmen. This was a departure from a philosophically perfect world and a move toward one that could function in the real world. His last dialogue, *Laws*, focuses on the Athenian Stranger and asks questions that point out the faulty arguments of others. During this time, Plato wrote down his views on issues ranging from how to build the perfect society to his ideas on love and the soul.

PLATO'S ACADEMY

The Academy was located in a grove of trees just outside the walls of Athens. The area, known as the Grove of Acadamy, was originally developed as a park. It had been the site of many religious festivals honoring the goddess Athena. The walled grounds, which were planted with olive trees, were also home to a large number of statues and temples. Plato owned a small garden on the property. It was here that he began to give his classes.

Plato's Academy trained philosophers and thinkers—most notably Aristotle—for more than nine hundred years until 529 CE, when Roman emperor Justinian closed it. Justinian claimed that the Academy and its teachers taught paganism, which soundly contrasted with his Christian faith. While Plato was still alive, he taught classes and supervised the other teachers who taught science, mathematics, philosophy, and government. There was a gymnasium on the property where students would engage in gymnastics and exercise, including wrestling, Plato's favorite sport. Plato accepted the enrollment of all who applied, including women.

Plato taught at the Academy for forty years until his death in 347 BCE. Because the teachers set school policy as a group, no one person had absolute power. This arrangement encouraged cooperation and allowed the Academy to change with the times. Plato composed many of his dialogues during his time at the Academy, including *The Republic*.

This engraving is called Plato and His Disciples in the Garden of the Academy. *It was drawn by Louis Figuier and engraved by Laplante, c. 1870.*

ARISTOTLE

Aristotle, Plato's most famous pupil, came to the Academy at the age of seventeen or eighteen c. 367 BCE. He was from Macedonia in the northeast part of what is now Greece. His father, Nichomachus, was Macedonian king Amyntas III's personal physician. Aristotle arrived while Plato was away visiting the court of Dionysius II in Sicily. Aristotle stayed at the Academy for twenty years, teaching there after his studies were completed. After Plato died in 347 BCE, Aristotle was passed over for leadership of the school, so he left the Academy and Athens.

Aristotle traveled first to Asia Minor in present-day Turkey and the island of Lesbos, where he tutored students and studied local plants

This bust depicts Aristotle, Plato's most famous student.

ARISTOTLE: EDUCATION AND LOGIC

Aristotle remained at the Academy for twenty years until the death of Plato. He is said to have left in disappointment at the new direction the Academy took after Plato's death. He became the head of an academy at Macedon and taught kings such as Alexander and Ptolemy. Alexander's determination to conquer Persia is said to have been heavily influenced by Aristotle. By 335 BCE, Aristotle had returned to Athens and founded his own school, where he taught for the next twelve years.

Aristotle is perhaps best known for a system of reasoning known as logic. Logic is the process of drawing conclusions from facts. A syllogism, or conclusion that can be made from two different premises, is one of Aristotle's most best-known concepts. For example:

All candy is sweet
Chocolate is candy
Therefore, chocolate is sweet

Aristotle's logic is an early ancestor of the scientific method, which governs the steps used during scientific experiments and research.

and animals. In 342 BCE, King Philip II of Macedonia hired Aristotle to tutor Alexander, his son and heir to the

A bronze relief of Alexander the Great shows him and his army in battle.

Macedonian throne. Aristotle taught Alexander grammar, politics, and literature, with special attention paid to the

Greek classics by Homer, *The Iliad* and *The Odyssey*, in addition to philosophy.

In 335 BCE, Aristotle returned to Athens and founded a school of his own known as the Lyceum. With generous financial contributions from Alexander, who ruled Macedonia after Philip's death in 336 BCE, Aristotle built enormous collections of both plant and animal specimens as well as a large library of maps and manuscripts at the Lyceum, which were used for research.

While Aristotle greatly admired Plato, many of Aristotle's original ideas and theories were in opposition to those of Plato's. For example, Aristotle readily disagreed with Plato's theory of the forms. Instead, he believed the world was observable through our senses of smell, taste, touch, sight, and sound. According to Aristotle, the only way to learn about the world was to study it scientifically, using a methodology that focused on using reason and scientific experiments. Aristotle made great strides in the sciences. Taxonomy—the science of classifying living organisms— was first developed by Aristotle, and his system is still the basis of categorization by biologists today.

UTOPIA

Plato based many of his ideas of a perfect society, or utopia, on Sparta, the city-state that conquered and ruled Athens during Plato's young adulthood. The entire Spartan society was geared toward war and defending itself against enemies, and Plato's utopia shared many of these properties.

In Plato's perfect society, no one had any personal possessions. Everything was held collectively by the state or the entire society. Plato conceived of a strict system of education and training that would eventually produce what he believed to be the best kind of ruler for his perfect society.

Like the Spartans, Plato believed that all children should be taken from their families and educated as a group. Plato reasoned that raising children apart from parents would instill in them the idea that the state was assuming the parental role as opposed to their biological

Amaurotū vibs.

Fons Anydri.

Ostium anydri

Thomas More, an English philosopher, wrote Utopia *in 1518 about an ideal state. This woodcut of the island of Utopia is from the first edition.*

mother and father. According to Plato, this would make the children loyal to the state and teach them that protecting it was their responsibility.

However, Plato's ideas differed from those of the Spartans in one very important way: he believed men and women were equal. This was a fairly radical idea for the time, but Plato practiced it in his own life, by teaching females as well as males at the Academy.

Plato believed that all people were born with certain abilities and that it was up to the leaders of the state to decide whether people would be best employed as farmers, businesspeople, soldiers, or rulers. Plato's utopia put its citizens through a rigorous educational program, separating them according to ability. Plato formulated a theory that explained his system of grouping people. His idea was that Earth was the true mother of all people. He believed that people were fashioned from certain metals, which would indicate their position in society.

He presented this idea of being born into a position in *The Republic*, stating that "in fashioning those of you who would be competent to rule" the gods "mixed gold in at their birth; this is why they are most honored; in auxiliaries (the military), silver; and iron and bronze in the farmers and the other craftsmen." In other words, people who were made primarily of gold, for example,

Plato believed in a strict class hierarchy, including the domination of people over animals. In this illustration, Plato is using music to charm wild animals.

خیال بست ناش بمیت نیت
چنان کا می کشیدی بنفس
چو و نبت الد سرکپی
چنان پیانت شر سیق زخزش
زقانون آن یا نحر کمی
برون شمصر او نتوش
دده دام از پا بافی کبو
همی مک از خوش نقت پاک

نه مجاکه زه مرد ور پا پیت
بقص طب خیر کشی میخش
بیت امش هو بتان سی
کزانده به اول دار ور پخش
زر علی بافت عقل کبی
بجر نبت انداز پاخش
روان کرو رخوه کروه ناکروه

نمان نیت او مثی دود
باغ به هما مم بران پانخت
رمویتی آور پا پی پن
بجای پی سید ابار کزنواخت
چوان زخنون بت یمام
خطی چا رکوکرز خوه رکشید
دویدند مرک کیک با آوازو

نگاه یک بران خذمیشرزد
کی کشت بدار و یک نخبت
کزارکشک پس خیا و نمون
که نا بار وبو بی علی مشتا
شان عم وخت بانو نام
دران خط شد وزخنون رکشید
فتاد نذ جون مرد رب ر وی خاک

would become the rulers, or guardians of the society; those made mostly from silver would be soldiers; and those made with mostly bronze and iron would be farmers and businesspeople.

Plato also stated that the social position of a child's parents did not automatically determine the position of the child. He wrote in *The Republic* that sometimes "a silver child will be born from a golden parent, a golden child from a silver parent, and similarly all the others from each other." Plato leaves room for every person in his utopia to rise or fall in status to his or her truest potential as a member of the society.

EDUCATION IN UTOPIA

In Plato's utopia, education would be initially concentrated in two areas: music and gymnastics. The study of music would include playing an instrument, singing, and poetry. Music and poetry would focus on the ideas of justice and the ability to be a good citizen of the state. The music would be military marches, which Plato believed helped promote love of the state. Music, drama, and poetry that did not deal with patriotic messages would be banned. Gymnastics would be studied to promote health and well-being as well as preparation for military training.

When young people reached the age of twenty, the students who showed the most academic promise would be selected to continue their educations. Meanwhile, those who did not would be trained to work as craftspeople, farmers, and businesspeople. Their role would be to support the entire society. For the next ten years, those who continued their studies would concentrate on the study of science and mathematics, including astronomy, geometry, and general arithmetic.

After ten years of science and math, the best students again would be separated into two groups based on their academic performance. Those who excelled would become politicians and would rule the state upon completing their educations. The others would be sent into careers in the military. The group of future politicians would study philosophy for the next five years, followed by fifteen years of education in government. Schooling would last until the students reached the age of fifty. Plato felt that they would be the only people whose capabilities could be relied upon to rule justly. In Plato's works, he doesn't indicate how many of these chosen philosopher-rulers would govern in his perfect state, but from this group, one supreme ruler would be chosen. This person would become what Plato termed the philosopher-king.

LIFE IN UTOPIA

The men and women rulers would live together in a dormitory-style arrangement. Marriage would not be permitted, although romantic love would not be banned. Marriage, Plato felt, was better left to those who were unworthy to rule—in other words, the farmers, businesspeople, and craftspeople who supported the society. Even in a marriage among the lower classes, the children would be separated from the parents. Plato felt that forcing his philosopher-rulers to live without personal attachments or possessions would make them impossible to corrupt since their loyalty would be first and foremost to the state.

People would be fed, clothed, and protected from harm, but the chief focus was keeping the society going. There would not be much advancement in culture or the arts, since all forms of culture that did not support or glorify the state would be banned. In Plato's utopia, the society would be well defended and self-sustaining, but many rights and privileges of individuals would be ignored in favor of the good of the society as a whole.

THE MAKING OF A PHILOSOPHER-KING

In 367 BCE, Plato's old friend Dion informed him that Dionysius I, the first ruler Plato tried to mold into his ideal philosopher-king, had recently died. His son Dionysius II had ascended to the throne. The boy's father had been so paranoid about his son stealing power that he imprisoned Dionysius II for most of his childhood. The younger Dionysius spent his days doing carpentry projects while he was completely excluded from his father's court.

Dion believed that a ruler who had not been exposed to the politics of the court was the ideal person to be molded into a true philosopher-king. Dion begged Plato to make a return journey to Italy. Plato, who was eager to test his ideas about the makings of an ideal ruler in the real world, consented and made the journey to Syracuse.

Unfortunately for Plato and Dion, their initial ideas about Dionysius II could not have been more wrong. The new king was surrounded by many of the same courtiers who had made his father's court such a dangerous place for both of them. Dionysius II's lack of experience made him easily controlled by these people. At the courtiers' urging, Dionysius II accused both Dion and Plato of treason. The young ruler banished his uncle Dion from the kingdom and forced Plato to stay in Syracuse against his will. Luckily for Plato, he was once again rescued by friends and returned to the safety of Athens and the Academy, where Dion was waiting for him.

Dionysius II, who was extremely upset that Plato had escaped Syracuse, kept sending word to Athens that he wanted Plato to return. The young king was in no position to explore any of Plato's ideas about utopia because Carthage was waging war against Syracuse in an attempt to conquer Italy. However, Dionysius II enjoyed the philosophical discussions and came to regard Plato as a sort of father figure. Dionysius II attempted to blackmail Plato into returning to Syracuse by threatening to seize all of Dion's possessions if Plato refused to return.

Eventually, Plato agreed to go back and help his friend. He sailed for Syracuse for a third time in 361 BCE. Once he arrived, he was again virtually a prisoner, to whom Dionysius II paid little attention. Once again, Plato had to rely on friends for an escape back to Athens. After a time, Dion returned to Syracuse,

This oil painting, The Sword of Damocles *by Felix Auvray, depicts the courtier Damocles, who exchanged places with Dionysius II but then discovered a sword hanging over his head. He then begged the king to switch back. The king had successfully illustrated that fortune and power comes with grave responsibility.*

dethroned his nephew, and ruled Syracuse until he was assassinated in 354 BCE.

Plato's inability to make either Dionysius I or Dionysius II into his ideal philosopher-king made him rethink his ideas of the ideal society. However, many of the aspects of Plato's utopia are present in government systems today. Communism and fascism exhibited many of the characteristics of Plato's utopia, including a strong government with a primary ruler who was supported by a group of political advisers, state-run defense, agriculture, and business programs, and the act of banning any art that criticized the state. The existence of these systems proves that Plato's utopia is possible in the real world, although the flaws of the system—in no small part due to the corruption of those in power—have made these political systems unappealing to most nations.

PLATONIC LOVE

In the *Symposium*, Plato took on what many scholars, philosophers, and artists consider to be the most complex subject of all—love. The *Symposium* takes place at a party in Athens where many of the city's cultural aristocracy (including Socrates) are gathered to celebrate Agathon's drama award for a tragedy he wrote. In the end of the *Symposium*, Plato has Socrates tell his colleagues that love is what draws us upward toward the forms. Plato believed that love was the soul's motivation toward goodness. According to Plato, physical or romantic attraction to another person was the lowest form of love. Plato believed that the impulse to love another unselfishly is the greatest act of which human souls are capable. The concept of loving someone in a nonromantic way has come to be known as Platonic love.

THE HUMAN SOUL

According to Plato, the soul of a human being was the core of a person's character. Plato believed that the soul was divided into three parts: the appetites, mind, and spirit. The mind prevented desires of both the appetites and spirit from overwhelming the soul. Without the mind to oversee it, the appetites would seek only passion and pleasure. According to Plato, these were the least honorable desires. The spirit represents all emotions, which drives a person to show courage and do great deeds. When a person's spirit is unbalanced, he or she can easily become overconfident and make serious blunders, which can lead to terrible consequences—even death.

In his dialogue the *Phaedrus*, Plato discusses the ability to control the objectionable appetites of the soul that can lead a person toward making an error. He states that "happiness depends on self-control." Many characters in Greek mythology exhibited these kinds of character defects, known as tragic flaws, which ultimately led them to make deadly mistakes. An example is the myth of Daedalus and Icarus, a father and son who were imprisoned in a tower on the island of Crete. Because the king monitored all ships leaving the island, Daedalus could not escape by sea. In search of a way out, he constructed two pairs of wings from feathers and wax. He then instructed Icarus on how to use them, telling him not to fly too close to the sun because the wax would melt and cause the wings to fall apart. However, Icarus did not listen to his father. He died because he had flown too close to the sun, which caused his wings to disintegrate. He gave in to his desire for pleasure, and as a result he lost his life. The myth of Icarus is an illustration of what can happen to a person who allows his or her emotions to overwhelm self-control.

PLATO'S LAWS

In his last dialogue, known as the *Laws*, Plato once again tackled the idea of building a society, as he had in *The Republic*. However, this time, he was less interested in a perfect society than one that would function in the real world. Socrates does not appear as a character in the *Laws*. Instead, Plato substituted him with the Athenian Stranger, who functions as Socrates did in previous dialogues by asking questions and pointing out the faulty arguments of others as he cleverly puts forth his own point of view. After he finished the *Laws*, in 347 BCE, Plato died at the age of eighty-one. He was buried at the Academy. Like his teacher Socrates, Plato dedicated his entire life to the pursuit of truth and wisdom.

Plato is depicted in the center of this famous fresco, The School of Athens, *by Raphael, which adorns a wall in the Vatican Museum.*

CONCLUSION

Like Socrates before him, Plato had the ability to make people think. This is perhaps why his work has enduring appeal and the reason it continues to be studied more than two thousand years after Plato's death. His theory of immutable forms continues to challenge those who study his philosophy. Scholars still question and debate exactly what the theory means and whether the theory is even feasible. Plato's influence extended beyond the world of philosophy to logic and mathematics, religion, and ethics. His work also influenced the creation of socio-political systems that did not exist in his time. The ideal communal society of *The Republic* was referenced and expanded by Sir Thomas More in his book *Utopia*, which described a communist, pagan state. After the Industrial Revolution of the late eighteenth and nineteenth centuries, communism gained popularity in Russia and spread to other countries around the world, often through force. Plato's glorification of state over all else likely influenced the kinds of propaganda posters that were used to support communist regimes.

Although used by communists to neutralize the concept of religion, Plato's theories were taken by some to represent religious ideals. St. Augustine (354–430), a Christian priest and theologian, believed that Plato's theory of the ideal forms represented heaven. Augustine thought that by understanding the true nature of forms, a person could have a greater understanding of God.

Plato's views on equality between the sexes, the perfect society, and the philosopher-ruler continue to generate discussion and study. Although living in Plato's utopia might not be particularly appealing to most people, the questions of how to create the best type of society, how to establish wise and incorruptible governance, and how to foster equality between the sexes are still hotly debated. Perhaps the most timeless of Plato's examinations is his never-ending search for truth above all else. This is a fundamental question of humankind, one that has been grappled with by every generation. "What is the truth?" is a question every person wants an answer to. The methods by which we attempt to examine and uncover truth keep the philosophies of Plato worth understanding.

TIMELINE

431 BCE The Peloponnesian War begins.

428/427 BCE Plato is born in Athens.

CIRCA 407 BCE Plato becomes a student of Socrates's.

404 BCE The Peloponnesian War ends in defeat for Athens; Sparta establishes an oligarchy, including a ruling party that came to be known as the Thirty Tyrants.

403 BCE Exiled enemies of the Thirty Tyrants raise armies in an attempt to restore democratic rule.

402 BCE The Thirty Tyrants are ousted. Democracy is reinstated in Athens.

399 BCE Socrates is tried and sentenced to death. Plato leaves Athens for Megara, Italy, and North Africa for twelve years.

395 BCE Plato develops an interest in mathematics, thanks to the work of Pythagoras.

388 BCE Plato's first visit to Syracuse in the court of Dionysius I. Dionysius attempts to have Plato sold into slavery on the island of Aegina, but Plato is miraculously rescued by a friend and returned to Athens.

387 BCE Plato founds the Academy in the Grove of Academus outside the city of Athens.

380 BCE Plato writes *The Republic*.

367 BCE Plato returns to Syracuse at the urging of Dion to tutor the young king Dionysius II.

366 BCE Aristotle becomes Plato's student.

360–361 BCE Plato visits the court of Dionysius II of Syracuse for the last time.

347 BCE Plato dies in Athens, at the age of eighty-one. He is buried at the Academy.

83 BCE The Academy finally closes after the death of Philo of Larissa, although philosophers continue to teach Plato's work.

410 CE The Academy reopens as a center for Neoplatonism.

529 CE The Academy is finally closed 900 years after it first opened, when Roman emperor Justinian I closes all philosophy schools.

GLOSSARY

AGORA The marketplace in Athens.

ALLEGORY A story in which characters and events represent ideas about politics, history, or life.

AUTOCRACY Rule by one person, such as a king, who is given absolute power over the people.

CHORUS A group of singers and dancers that commented on the action of a Greek play.

COMMUNISM A political and societal system in which the government owns all facets of industry and there are no privately owned possessions.

DEMOCRACY A political system in ancient Greece that gave each citizen of the city-state the right to vote on policy.

DIALOGUES Discussions between two or more characters.

EPIC POETRY Poems that tell the story of the deeds of a great hero or heroes.

ETHICS A system of moral values or principles.

FASCISM A system of government in which a society is ruled by a dictator and there is no free speech.

FORMS Objects or ideas outside of human experience that can be understood only through the mind.

HELOT A Spartan slave.

HEMLOCK A poisonous drink made from a plant with small white flowers.

HYPOTENUSE The side opposite the right angle of a right triangle.

METICS Free men who had immigrated to Athens.

METROPOLITAN Relating to a large city or urban area.

OBVERSE A coin or medal with the head of a person on one side.

OLIGARCHY Government by a small group of the rich and powerful that makes policy decisions for all.

ORACLES Sacred beings who had the ability to see into the future.

ORCHESTRA Roughly translates to "the dancing place," a circle of ground where plays were performed.

PAGAN One who follows a polytheistic religion.

PHILOSOPHER One who seeks thought and wisdom.

PHILOSOPHY The pursuit of wisdom.

PLATONIC LOVE Loving someone in a nonromantic way.

POLIS A city-state in ancient Greece.

POLYTHEISTIC Referring to the worship of multiple gods.

PYTHAGOREAN A follower of the teachings of Pythagoras.

RELATIVISM The belief that things may be true or right for different people at different times.

SOPHISTS Teachers who traveled through Greece teaching classes for a fee.

SYLLOGISM A conclusion that can be made from two different ideas that are true.

TYRANT A leader who uses his power in a mean or cruel way.

UTOPIA A perfect society.

FOR MORE INFORMATION

American Philosophical Association
University of Delaware
31 Amstel Avenue
Newark, DE 19716-4797
(30) 831-1112
Website: http://www.apaonline.org
The American Philosophical Association supports
  the professional development of philosophers
  and promotes the discipline and profession of
  philosophy.

American Philosophical Society
104 South Fifth Street
Philadelphia, PA 19106-3387
(215) 440-3400
Website: http://www.amphilsoc.org
A scholarly organization that promotes knowledge
  of the sciences and humanities through research,
  library resources, publications, and professional
  meetings.

Association for Informal Logic & Critical Thinking
Center for Critical Thinking
Baker University
Baldwin City, KS 66006
Website: https://ailact.wordpress.com

This nonprofit organization promotes the teaching
of, research into, and testing of informal logic.

The Canadian Philosophical Association
Saint Paul University
223 Main Street
Ottawa, ON K1S 1C4
Canada
(613) 236-1393, x2454
Website: http://www.acpcpa.ca
Founded in 1958, this association promotes
philosophical scholarship and education in
Canada.

Canadian Society for Continental Philosophy
The University of Calgary
2500 University Drive N.W.
Calgary, AB T2N 1N4
Canada
Website: http://www.c-scp.org/en
The CSCP is dedicated to the pursuit and exchange
of philosophical ideas and provides a forum for
scholarly interests in the field of philosophy.

International Plato Society (IPS)
Gabriele Cornelli

Archai Unesco Chair

University of Brasília

70904-970,

Brasília, DF

Brazil

Website: http://platosociety.org

The International Plato Society promotes
Platonic studies throughout the world and
communication among scholars of diverse
disciplines working on Plato. It organizes
symposia and promotes the publication of books
and scholarly articles on Plato.

International Society for Neoplatonic Studies

United States Section

John F. Finamore, President

Department of Classics

210 Jefferson Building

University of Iowa

Iowa City, Iowa 52242

(319) 335-0288

Email: john-finamore@uiowa.edu

Website: http://www.isns.us/us.htm

The International Society for Neoplatonic Studies is an international collection of philosophers, classicists, cultural historians, and other scholars interested in the historical significance and contemporary relevance of Neoplatonic thought.

Society for Philosophy and Psychology (SPP)
Department of Philosophy
206 McMicken Hall
University of Cincinnati
Cincinnati, OH 45221-037
Website: http://socphilpsych.org
The SPP is a North American educational organization that promotes interaction between philosophers, psychologists, and other cognitive scientists.

WEBSITES

Because of the changing nature of Internet links, Rosen Publishing has developed an online list of websites related to the subject of this book. This site is updated regularly. Please use this link to access the list:

http://www.rosenlinks.com/GGP/Plato

FOR FURTHER READING

Buckingham, Will. *The Philosophy Book* (Big Ideas Simply Explained). New York, NY: DK Publishing, 2011.

Ferry, Luc. *The Wisdom of the Myths: How Greek Mythology Can Change Your Life*. New York, NY: Harper Perennial, 2014.

Goldstein, Rebecca. *Plato at the Googleplex: Why Philosophy Won't Go Away*. New York, NY: Pantheon, 2014.

Hall, Edith. *Introducing the Ancient Greeks: From Bronze Age Seafarers to Navigators of the Western Mind*. New York, NY: W. W. Norton & Company, 2014.

Herman, Arthur. *The Cave and the Light: Plato Versus Aristotle, and the Struggle for the Soul of Western Civilization*. New York, NY: Random House, 2013.

Hughes, Bettany. *The Hemlock Cup: Socrates, Athens and the Search for the Good Life*. New York, NY: Vintage Books, 2012.

Johnson, Shelly. *The Argument Builder*. Camp Hill, PA: Classical Academic Press, 2008.

Larsen, Aaron, and Joelle Jodge. *The Art of Argument*. Camp Hill, PA: Classical Academic Press, 2010.

Law, Stephen. *Philosophy Rocks!* New York, NY:
Volo Books, 2002.

Plato, and C. D. C. Reeve, ed. *A Plato Reader: Eight
Essential Dialogues*. Indianapolis, IN: Hackett
Publishing Company, Inc., 2012.

Plato. *The Republic*. Mineola, NY: Dover
Publications, 2000.

Taylor, A. E. *Plato: The Man and His Work*. Mineola,
NY: Dover Publications, Inc., 2011.

BIBLIOGRAPHY

Baker, Rosalie F., and Charles F. Baker III. *Ancient Greeks: Creating the Classical Tradition*. Oxford, England: Oxford University Press, 1997.

Bio. "Plato." Retrieved November 19, 2014 (http://www.biography.com/people/plato-9442588).

Buchanan, Scott, ed. *The Portable Plato*. New York, NY: Penguin, 1977.

Cavalier, Robert. *Plato for Beginners*. New York, NY: Writers and Readers Publishing, Inc., 1998.

Eshleman, Kendra. *The Social World of Intellectuals in the Roman Empire: Sophists, Philosophers, and Christians*. New York, NY: Cambridge University Press, 2012.

Freeland, Cynthia. "Ancient Greek Philosophy: Philosophy 3383." University of Houston. Retrieved January 2005 (http://www.uh.edu/~cfreelan/courses/plato.html).

Goldstein, Rebecca. *Plato at the Googleplex: Why Philosophy Won't Go Away*. Evansville, IN: Vintage, 2015.

Herman, Arthur. *The Cave and the Light: Plato Versus Aristotle, and the Struggle for the Soul of Western Civilization*. New York, NY: Random House, 2014.

Kraut, Richard. "Plato." *The Stanford Encyclopedia of Philosophy*, Fall 2013 edition. Retrieved November 19, 2014 (http://plato.stanford.edu/archives /fall2013/entries/plato/).

Loverance, Rowena, and Tim Wood. *Ancient Greece.* New York, NY: Viking, 1992.

Plato. *Complete Works.* John M. Cooper, D. S. Hutchinson, Eds. Cambridge, MA: Hackett Publishing Co., 1997.

Plato. *The Last Days of Socrates.* Harold Tarrant, Ed. Hugh Tredennick, Trans. New York, NY: Penguin, 2003.

Plato. *The Republic.* Allan Bloom, trans. New York, NY: Basic Books, 1991.

Powell, Anton. *Cultural Atlas for Young People: Ancient Greece.* New York, NY: Facts on File, 2003.

INDEX

ABOUT THE AUTHORS

Lindsay Zoubek is a philosophy and theology student and writer living in Knoxville, TN. While her study focuses on women philosophers, she believes that much is owed to Western philosophy's founding fathers, Socrates and Plato.

Alex Sniderman came to his interest in Plato and Greek philosophy from his research for this book. Mr. Sniderman is following in the footsteps of his great-grandfather R.M. Wenley, who came from Scotland to be the first chairman of the philosophy department of the University of Michigan, Ann Arbor. Mr. Sniderman lives in Brooklyn, NY.

PHOTO CREDITS